Dear Geoff and Kathy — Libby and I enjoyed every minute of our visit with you immensely! Thank you for everything! We love you and your wonderful family. We do so very much hope we meet again sooner rather than later.

[signature]
June 2, 2025

Charlotte
NORTH CAROLINA

A PHOTOGRAPHIC PORTRAIT

Photography by Patrick Schneider

Narrative by Lore Postman Schneider

TWIN LIGHTS PUBLISHERS | ROCKPORT, MASSACHUSETTS

Copyright © 2017 by
Twin Lights Publishers, Inc.

All rights reserved. No part of this book may be reproduced in any form without written permission of the copyright owners. All images in this book have been reproduced with the knowledge and prior consent of the artists concerned and no responsibility is accepted by producer, publisher, or printer for any infringement of copyright or otherwise, arising from the contents of this publication. Every effort has been made to ensure that credits accurately comply with information supplied.

First published in the
United States of America by:

Twin Lights Publishers, Inc.
Rockport, Massachusetts 01966
Telephone: (978) 546-7398
www.twinlightspub.com

ISBN: 978-1-934907-49-8

10 9 8 7 6 5 4 3 2 1

(opposite)
Marshall Park

(frontispiece)
Charlotte Skyline

(jacket front)
Evening Skyline

(jacket back)
First Ward Park and Uptown

Book design by:
SYP Design & Production, Inc.
www.sypdesign.com

Printed in China

Charlotte is a city of purposeful newcomers – many of them individuals who compared Charlotte to their current addresses and said, "Let's pack up the moving van!"

This influx of new residents has changed the Charlotte metro area in powerful ways. New neighborhoods sprung up and stretched out along Charlotte's perimeter. Closer to Uptown, stately homes replaced tiny bungalows along the tree-lined streets of Myers Park, Historic Dilworth, and other nearby neighborhoods. The populations of its outskirt communities like Huntersville and Cornelius to the north, and Pineville and Waxhaw to the south quickly doubled in size.

With this growing population came world-class amenities that make Charlotte an inviting and captivating place. There are can't-miss museums for every interest and curiosity; easily accessible professional sports teams; entertainment venues that offer music, dance, and performances; roughly three dozen colleges and universities; more than 200 county parks and miles of greenways that beckon visitors on bike and by foot; Retailers and restaurants; a vibrant airport, and new buildings that have changed the Uptown skyline with ever-taller skyscrapers. And so much more.

Despite its growth, Charlotte remains a big city with small-town charm. A place where strangers on the street nod or say hello, and even harried Uptown workers will stop to offer directions for tourists. This modern, melting-pot city embraces and helps newcomers fit in and continues to be a welcoming place to visit and call home. On the following pages, Patrick Schneider's photography takes readers on a visual journey that makes it easy to see why so many choose to call Charlotte home.

Evening Skyline *(opposite)*

Charlotte's ever-changing skyline is a constant reminder of the city's popularity. At the city's center is its tallest building, the 60-story Bank of America Corporate Center. Since its completion in 1992, the 871-foot tower has remained the city's tallest building even as two dozen skyscrapers have grown up around it.

Sunset Reflections (top)

Bank of America Corporate Center, one of several structures housing employees of the nation's second-largest bank, is reflected in a nearby building at sunset. Its crown-shaped spire helps the building—and city—stand out architecturally. The glass spires are illuminated from within and can change colors.

Bank of America Corporate Center (bottom)

Located at the heart of Uptown Charlotte, Bank of America Corporate Center is the tallest building between Philadelphia and Atlanta. Long-time residents sometimes call it the "Taj McColl" after former Bank of America CEO Hugh McColl, who was responsible for the tower's construction.

Duke Energy Center (opposite)

Visible from 20 miles away, the Duke Energy Center—Charlotte's second-tallest building—adds personality to the city's skyline. Most notable is the handle-shaped crown that glows each night and can change color with a few clicks on a computer. The Duke Energy Center was completed in 2010.

Metalmorphosis

Considered one of the Seven Wonders of Charlotte, the futuristic *Metalmorphosis* sculpture captivates visitors at the Whitehall Technology Park in southwest Charlotte. Created by Czech artist David Černý, the sculpture is made of spinning stainless-steel plates that form and reform into the shape of a giant metal head.

Hearst Tower *(above)*

An architecturally distinctive building that displays its own style even as it complements the design elements of surrounding structures, the 47-story Hearst Tower opened in 2002 as the city's third-tallest skyscraper. The tower gets its dramatic color variations from the pigments used in the precast concrete façade.

Romare Bearden Park *(pages 10–11)*

Named for Charlotte-born artist Romare Bearden, this 5.4-acre public park opened in 2013, across from BB&T Ballpark in Uptown Charlotte. The park's design is based on Bearden's collages and paintings. It features two gardens, a green field, interactive play areas, and dramatic waterfalls that welcome visitors.

Harvey B. Gantt Center *(above and left)*

Formerly known as the Afro-American Cultural Center, the center was renamed in honor of Harvey B. Gantt, the city's first African-American mayor. The four-story modernist glass-and-metal structure is a striking part of the Levine Center for the Arts on South Tryon Street.

Charlotte Convention Center *(above)*

Located on the south side of Uptown Charlotte, the Charlotte Convention Center is the city's premier meeting and convention space. The 550,000-square-foot structure was the first in North Carolina to "go green" with energy-saving initiatives, environmentally friendly cleaning products, and recycling programs.

Mecklenburg County Courthouse *(right)*

Over a span of 241 years, Charlotte has been home to eight courthouses serving Mecklenburg County. The newest courthouse was dedicated in 2007. The courtrooms and departments are organized around a central atrium, which soars six stories and provides abundant natural light.

The Writer's Desk
(above, left, and opposite)

In the plaza outside ImaginOn in Uptown, life-size typewriter keys, a pen quill, a giant pencil, and stacked stone books honor Rolfe Neill, a longtime publisher of the Charlotte Observer. Created by Larry Kirkland, the sculpture encourages children to jump from key to key.

Queen Charlotte of Mecklenburg (opposite)

A statue of Queen Charlotte stands outside Wake Forest University Charlotte Center in Uptown Charlotte. The city and county were named in honor of Princess Charlotte of Mecklenburg-Strelitz, who was married to King George III shortly before the county was formed in 1763.

Seventh Street Station (above)

A Lynx light rail train pauses near Seventh Street Station in Uptown. The nine-story parking garage is clad in a syncopated pattern of colored panels that create a lively and dynamic surface while also camouflaging the structure's mass. The building is home to restaurants and the 7th Street Public Market.

At Peace, At Play (above and left)

Painted steel oak trees and playful animals welcome visitors to a peaceful green space in the 500 block of N. Tryon Street Uptown. The works by North Carolina artist Joseph Miller were commissioned in 1998 as part of the Bank of America Art Collection.

Flying Shuttles (opposite)

Charlotte celebrates its textile mill roots and celebrates the Piedmont's craft and cotton tradition with four 50-foot-tall giant bobbins outside the Spectrum Center arena in Uptown. Created by artist Andrew Leicester, the pieces were installed in 2006.

Life is an Open Book *(above)*

Stone children climb on a giant brick book statue in The Green, a 1.5-acre pocket park tucked between the Charlotte Convention Center and the Levine Center for the Arts on South Tryon Street. The Green is home to numerous fountains and statues, landscaped walkways, motion-activated stone walls, and more.

Zygos *(opposite)*

At the corner of Trade and Poplar streets Uptown, the 21-foot-high *Zygos* sculpture is a striking example of a private company collaborating with the city's Arts and Science Council to create public art. The stainless steel sculpture was installed in 2007.

The Garden

The 30-foot-tall, multi-colored sculpture *The Garden* was unveiled in 1990 in a plaza along West Trade Street. Artist Jerry Peart made the piece of painted aluminum. In the decades since the sculpture was installed, hundreds of other works of art have been added to Charlotte's streets, both Uptown and beyond.

Ascendus

Feathers and wings inspired the 60-foot-tall steel and glass *Ascendus* sculpture that many travelers pass on their way to the Charlotte Douglas International Airport. Installed in 2012, the piece was created by artist Ed Carpenter to suggest an excitement of flight and ascent.

Statues at the Square *(above, left, and right)*

Charlotte has four statues on the corners of Trade Street and Tryon Street in Uptown. American sculptor Raymond Kaskey created the four public art statues to represent future, industry, transportation, and commerce.

Statues on the Square *(opposite and right)*

The figure of a gold miner spilling money on the head of a banker, represents commerce, while the sledge hammer-yielding railroad builder represents transportation. Some people say the face of the banker is modeled after Federal Reserve Chairman Alan Greenspan.

25

Evening Skyline *(above)*

A dramatic sky swirls over Charlotte at dusk. The skyline has changed significantly since the city's tallest building, Bank of America Corporate Center, opened in 1992. The third-tallest building, Hearst Tower (far left) opened in 2002, while the Duke Energy Center (far right) was completed in 2010.

South End *(opposite)*

A LYNX Blue Line light rail train passes through the city's historic South End. Charlotte began light rail service in 2007 with trains traveling a 9.6-mile route between Uptown and Pineville. LYNX operators, The Charlotte Area Transit System, or CATS, have continued to expand light rail service.

Skyline *(pages 28-29)*

Depending on your point of view, the Duke Energy Center (far left) can resemble a martini glass, the world's biggest cheese grater, a giant crystal, or a rocket waiting to blast off. Eighteen buildings with 20 or more floors have joined the Charlotte skyline since 2000.

Wells Fargo Atrium (top)
A bronze statue of a child at play contrasts giant tree ornaments balancing in the Wells Fargo Plaza on South Tryon Street. The boy is part of a larger piece of children playing in a cascading fountain, which was created by artists Dennis Smith and David Wagner.

Carolina Panthers (bottom)
Outside Bank of America Stadium, a Panther's statue roars in the winter holidays while adorned with a wreath and bow. The stadium has six identical bronze statues, which flank the facility's three main entrances. All are named *Indomitable Spirit* and were installed in 1996.

Singing Christmas Tree (opposite)
For more than 60 years, volunteer members of Carolina Voices form a 32-foot-tall singing Christmas tree to entertain audiences in the Knight Theater. Though Carolina Voices perform all year, the organization is best known for its Singing Christmas Tree performances.

First Ward Park *(above and opposite)*

Charlotte's 4-acre First Ward Park opened in late 2015. Located between ImaginOn and UNC Charlotte Center City building, the park redefines the First Ward community. Much of the land on which the park was built were previously surface parking lots.

Creative Seating *(left)*

Larger-than-life animals, carved in stone, form benches and creative sitting areas for visitors to First Ward Park. The friendly critters include a fox, an owl, and a rabbit. The park also includes flowerbeds, a rain garden, and a spacious lawn for recreation and concerts.

First Ward Park

Children play in jets of dancing water near an elaborate rock formation in the First Ward Park. As one of Charlotte's newest urban parks, the area is expected to spark major redevelopment of the city's First Ward area, much of which is still surface parking.

Ainsa III

Barcelona artist Jaume Plensa used letters from nine international alphabets to create a stainless-steel sculpture near the UNC Charlotte Center City building and First Ward Park. The seated figure was commissioned by the philanthropic group, Queen's Table, which has helped to beautify Charlotte's public spaces for 30 years.

The Green *(top and bottom)*

Three giant, stone fish spurt water on willing visitors to The Green, a 1.5-acre pocket park in Uptown. Stories come to life in this quirky, literary-themed wonderland, where children of all ages can jump hopscotch, solve puzzles, and discover public art treasures.

36

Little Sugar Creek Greenway

Midtown Park is part of the Little Sugar Creek Greenway, a public park with more than 19 miles of trails and land connectors. Until recently, this one-acre parcel was home to a gas station. Today the park's use of stone, artwork, and other materials brings new life to the area.

Little Sugar Creek Greenway
(above and left)

Charlotte designed the Sugar Creek Greenway with the goal of connecting neighborhoods, landmarks and activities, and increasing the Queen City's pedestrian-oriented activities. The greenway provides environmental benefits such as improved water quality through stream buffering, wildlife habitats, and flood control.

Sight Unseen *(opposite)*

The gleaming sphere *Sight Unseen* was installed in 2012 to bring visual art enjoyment to the sight-impaired. Artists Po Shu Wang and Louise Bertelsen blended Braille-embossed dots with modified music box readers to create five multi-dimensional pieces, described by the artists as Braille music boxes.

39

Warmth of Summer

A lovely young lady can't help but smile as her photo is taken among bunches of cheerful blooms in one of the many sunflower fields that blanket North Carolina each summer. This field is located on a farm in Weddington, located to the south of Uptown.

Swinging Charlotte Lifestyle

The late-afternoon sun casts a golden glow on a young boy as he swings on an old tire strung from a stately oak. This idyllic setting is located at Berewick, one of the many large-scale master planned communities built around Charlotte to house the city's growing population.

Freedom Park *(top and bottom)*

Charlotte's 98-acre Freedom Park, located in the historic Dilworth and Myers Park neighborhood, is well known for its paved trails and stone bridge over the 7-acre lake at the park's center. Freedom Park is named to honor the service and sacrifice of Mecklenburg County veterans.

Grandiflora *(opposite)*

Grandiflora, its name taken from the Latin name for southern magnolia, suggests the seedpods and graceful petals on the magnolia trees that are planted nearby. Located on the corner of Randolph and Wendover roads, artist Thomas Sayre was privately commissioned to create this unique sculpture in 2000.

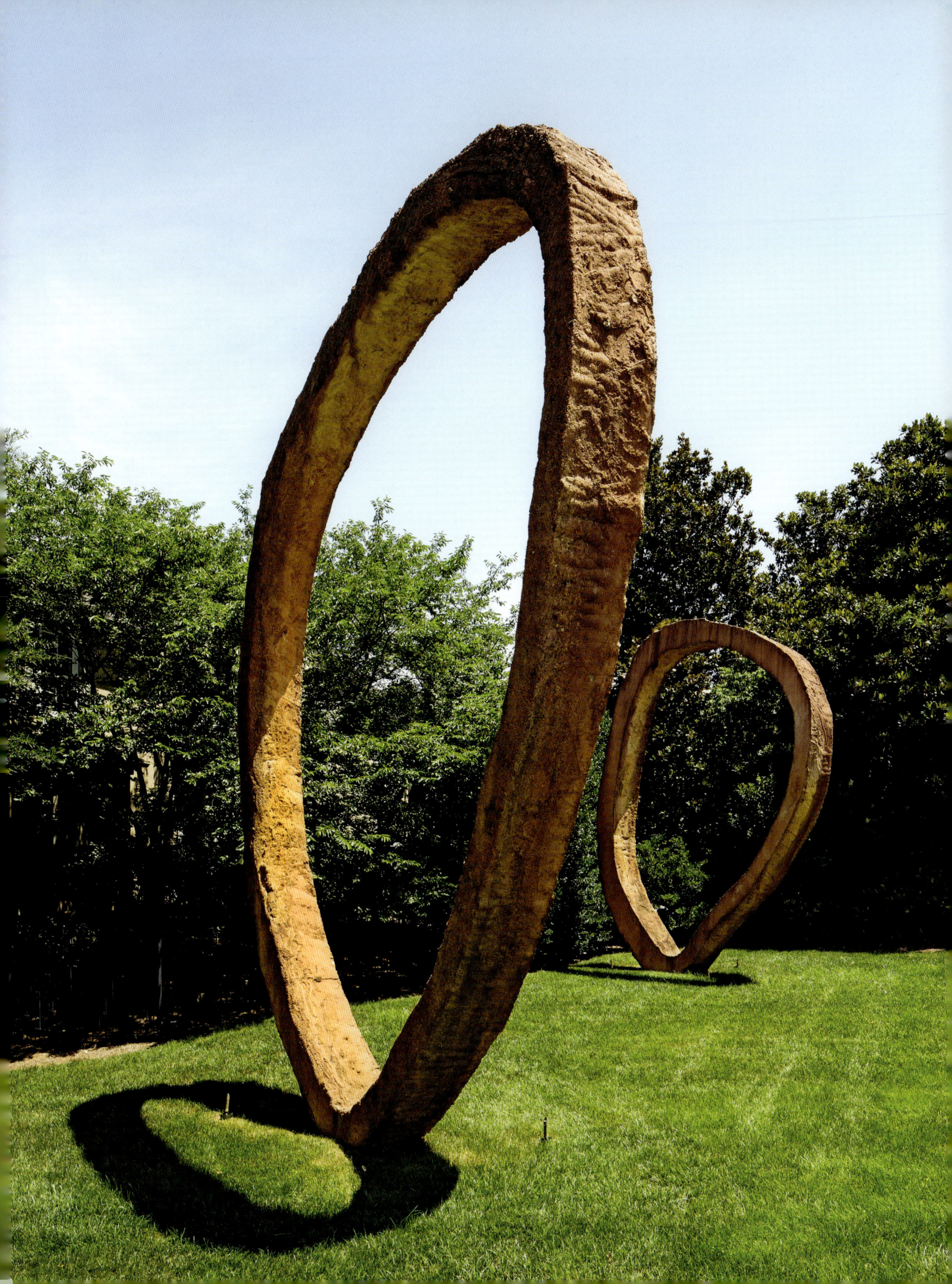

24 Hours of Booty *(above and left)*

Each July, approximately 1,200 cyclists take to the Myers Park streets for 24 Hours of Booty, a fundraiser for cancer research. The 3-mile Booty Loop runs through the Myers Park community. Participants ride for 24 hours as they raise funds and awareness.

Myers Park *(top)*

Myers Park is known for its stately homes, tree-lined streets, and odd intersections, including Queens/Queens and Providence/Providence. Developed after 1911, John Myers transformed a portion of his cotton farm into this elegant suburb adding willow, oak, elm, and poplar trees. Today it is a national historic district.

Old Man Traffic *(bottom)*

The 4-foot bronze statue that appears to be directing traffic in the middle of Queens Road near Providence Road was created in honor of Hugh McManaway, a Charlottean who grew up nearby and spent his later years directing traffic for enjoyment. His family commissioned the piece after his death in 1989.

Ragan Reflecting Canal

Fantastical fish appear to leap gracefully from the stream of the Ragan Reflecting Canal water feature at the Daniel Stowe Botanical Garden. The Ragan Reflecting Canal was donated in memory of Jocelyn Sikes Ragan. The feature stretches the length of a football field and is framed by a fountain at each end.

Daniel Stowe Botanical Garden
(top and bottom)

Spectacular gardens, a tropical plant conservatory, peaceful pathways, and captivating fountains allow visitors to reconnect with nature and glean ideas and inspiration. The 380-acre center near Lake Wylie was created by retired textile executive Daniel Stowe to provide beauty and joy for generations.

Orchid Conservatory (pages 48-49)

The five-story, 8,000-square-foot Orchid Conservatory at Daniel Stowe Botanical Garden is dedicated to displaying orchids and tropical plants in ever-changing exhibits. It's the crown jewel of the garden, which has built a substantial reputation in and around the Carolinas.

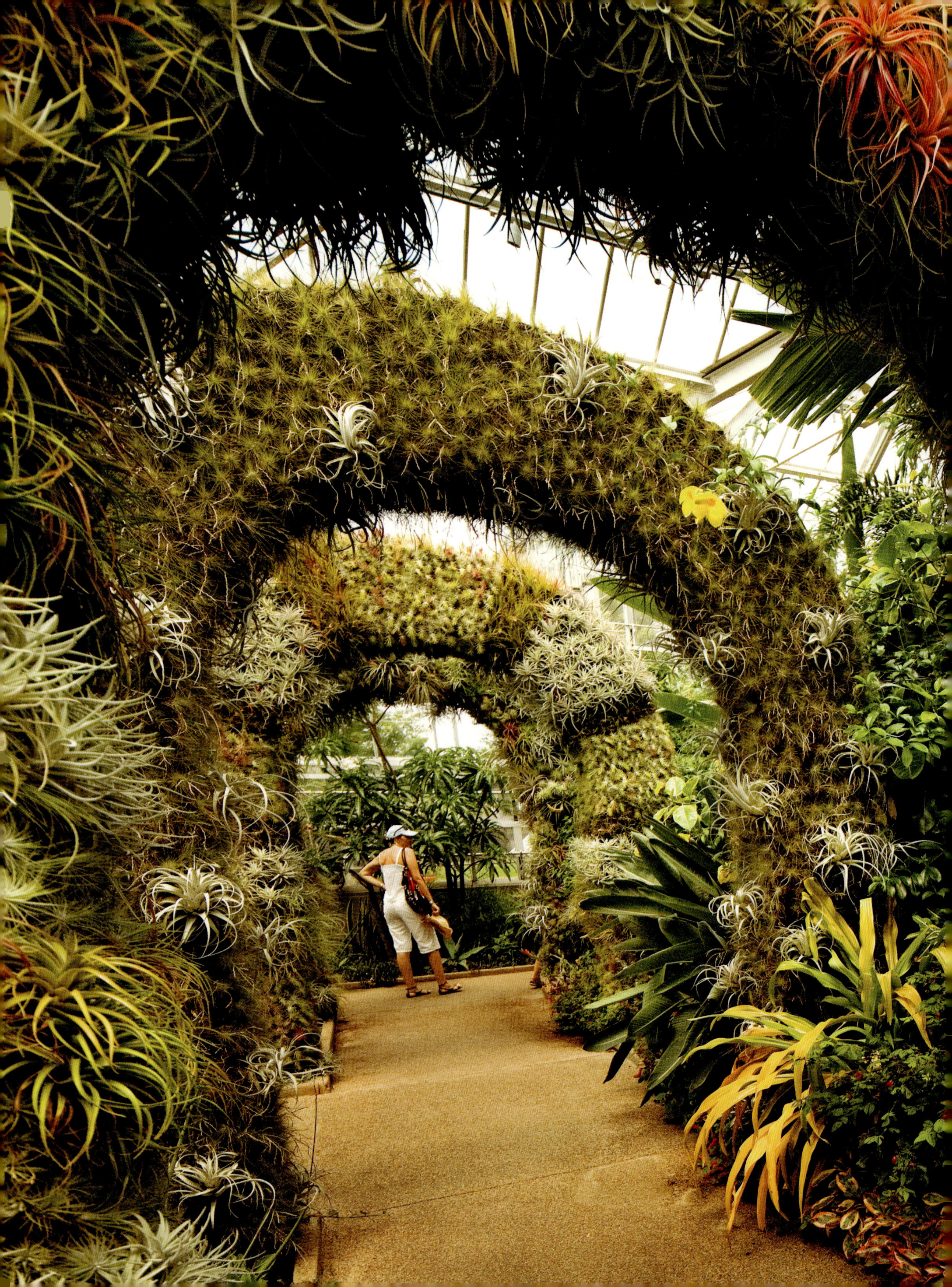

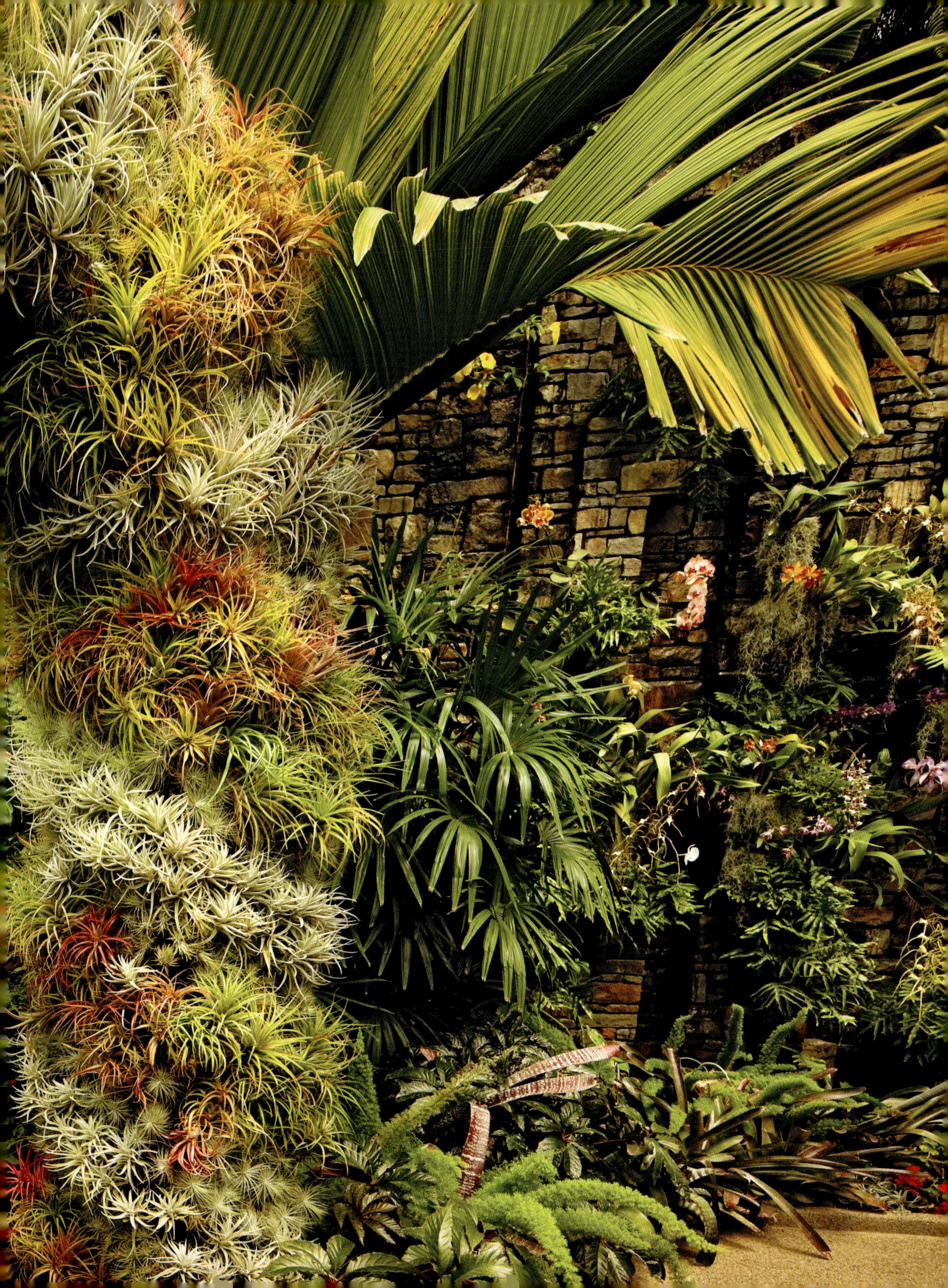

McGill Rose Garden *(above and left)*

In 1950, Charlotte philanthropist Henry McGill purchased the 1.4-acre site of a former coal and ice yard on North Davidson Street. Little by little, Helen McGill planted roses and transformed the former industrial site into a magnificent garden, which the couple eventually opened to the public to enjoy.

The Art of Nature

Tucked between the Garden District of First Ward and NoDa, Charlotte's historic arts district, the McGill Rose Garden provides bursts of color and welcoming whimsy. The garden has 1,000 roses, including 230 varieties, and many interesting statues and sculptures beckoning visitors to sit a while.

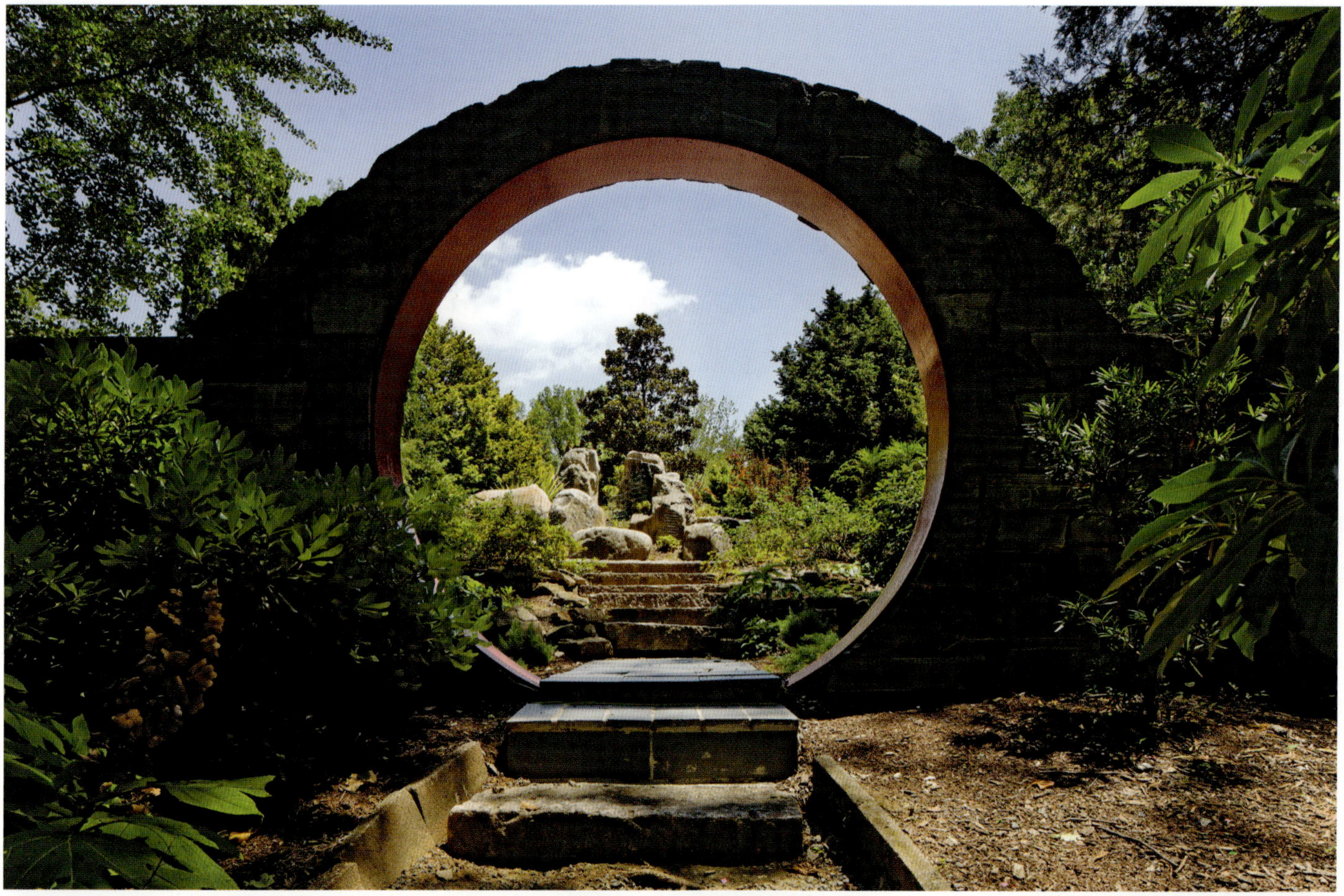

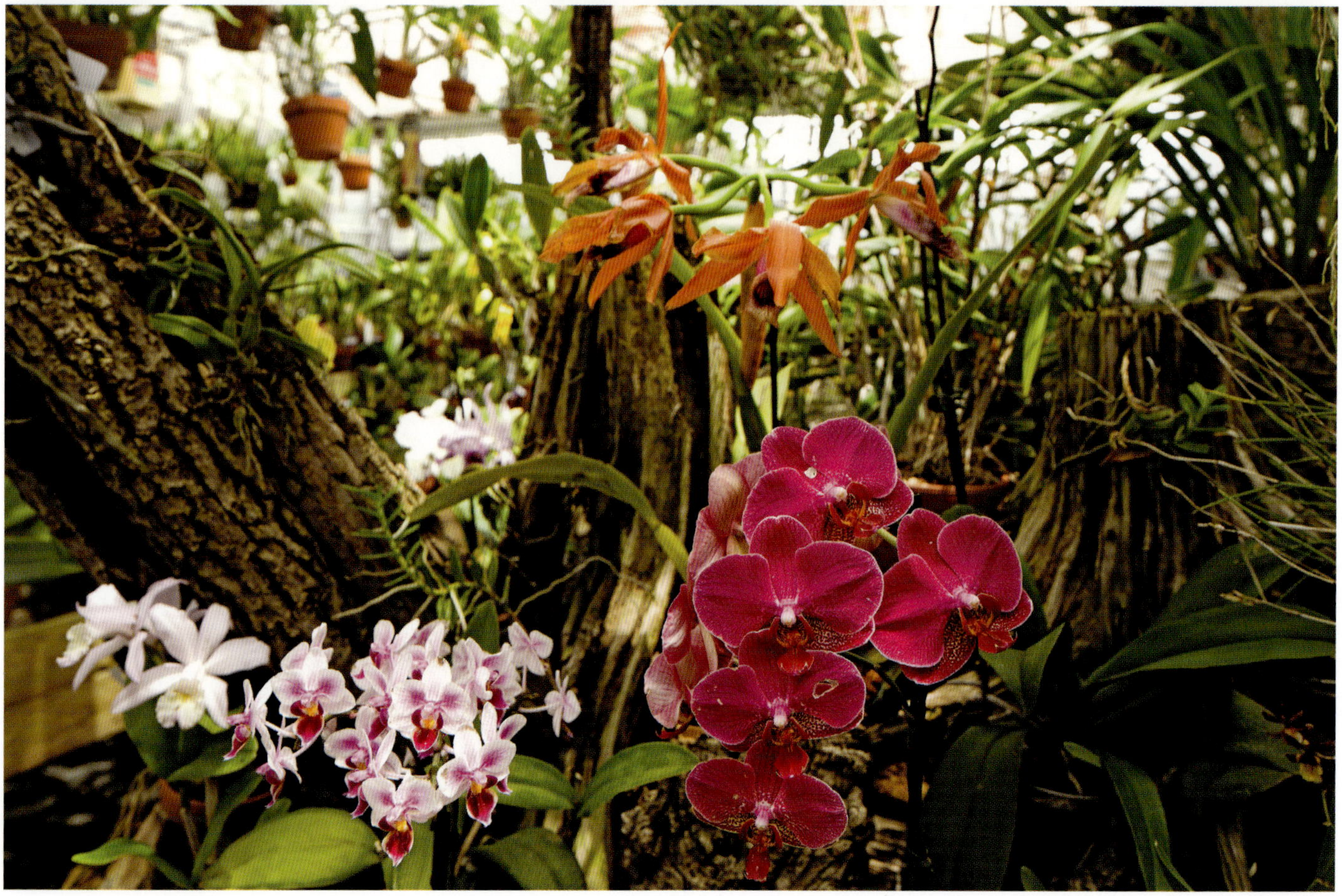

UNC Charlotte Botanical Gardens
(opposite top and bottom)

In its three garden sites, the UNC Charlotte Botanical Gardens hold curated collections of plants for inventory, education, conservation, research, and inspiration. The gardens include the eight-room McMillan Greenhouse, native woodlands, and a variety of manicured gardens with hardscapes.

Dinosaur Garden *(above)*

A full-sized Deinonychus skeleton sculpture welcomes all to the Dinosaur Garden, which features flora and fauna from a prehistoric world. This garden is part of UNC Charlotte's 4,000-square-foot McMillan Greenhouse. Other rooms feature carnivorous and bog plants, dessert succulents, orchids, and more.

53

University of North Carolina Charlotte *(above, left, and opposite)*

UNC Charlotte is home to more than 28,700 students studying for bachelors, masters, or doctoral degrees. A bronze statue of the 49er Gold Miner, UNC Charlotte's mascot, recalls the region's history as a gold-mining center and symbolizes the pioneering spirit and determination that has fueled the university's growth.

55

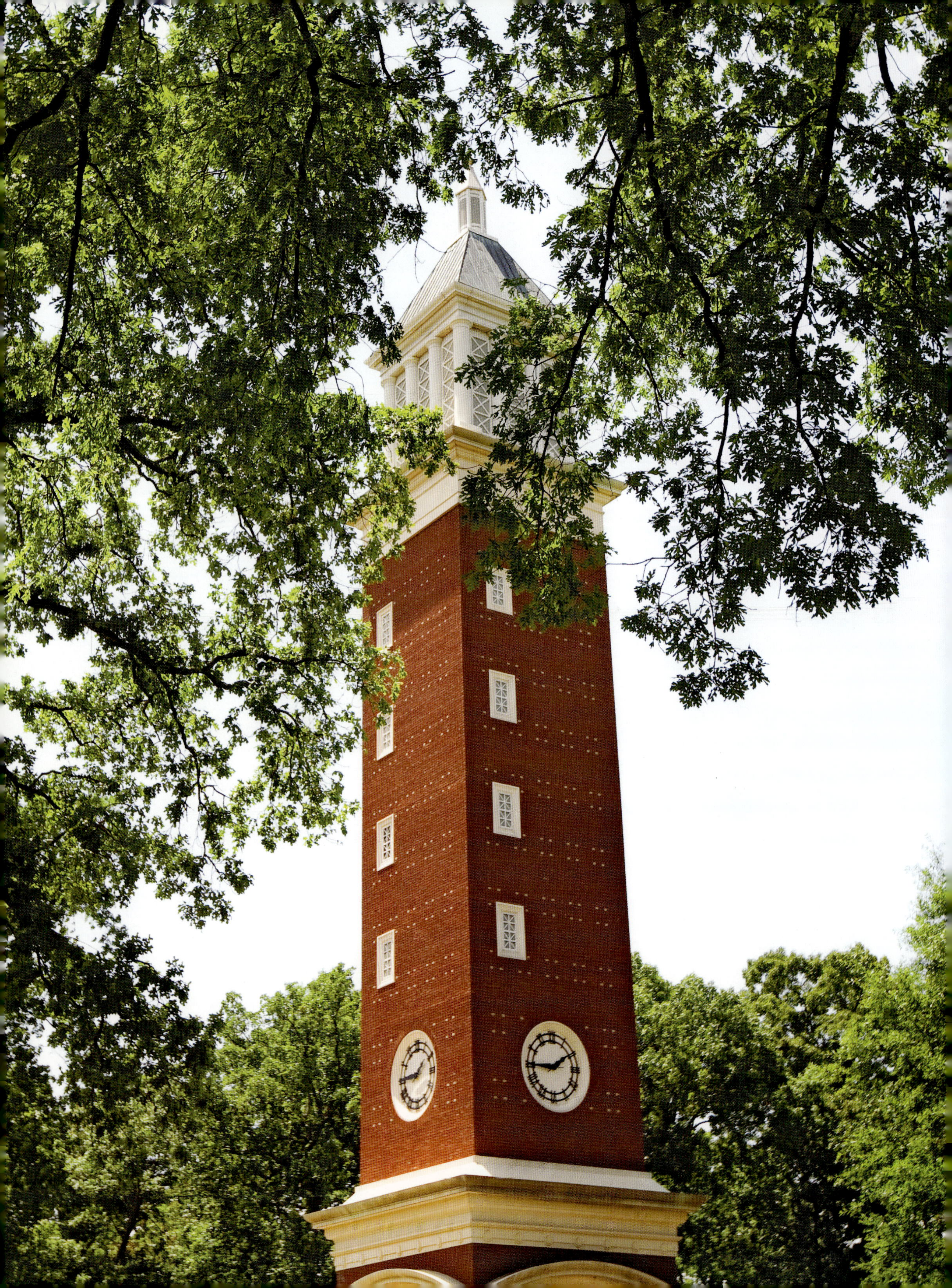

Queen University (opposite)

The iconic Evans Clock Tower welcomes visitors to Charlotte's Queens University, a private co-educational institution founded in 1857. Originally run as a college for women, Queens became co-educational in 1987. The school changed its name from Queens College to Queens University of Charlotte in 2002.

Miss Anne & Dan at Queens University (above)

A life-size copper and bronze sculpture forever commemorates Anne Beatty McKenna, a 1948 Queens graduate who passed away in 1999 and left the sculpture to her alma mater. Artist Elsie Shaw created the piece in a style that matched her *Old Man Traffic* sculpture.

Mecklenburg County Vietnam Veterans Memorial

A 270-foot-long granite arc, honoring Vietnam veterans from Mecklenburg County, is shaded by massive oak trees in Thompson Park, near Uptown. The granite panels offer a historical timeline, a war-time map of Southeast Asia, and names of the 105 Mecklenburg County veterans who died.

Mecklenburg County WWI Memorial

Now nearly 100 years old, this memorial honoring the brave veterans of WWI has stood in multiple sites around Charlotte before resting at its current location, on the lawn at City Hall on Fourth Street. The statue, called "Johnny Doughboy" by some locals, is made from pressed copper.

Mecklenburg County WWII Memorial

This WWII monument is located at the main entrance to Evergreen Cemetery on Central Avenue. It is dedicated to the memory of the 5,170 WWII dead who rested in the area before they were returned to their loved ones by the American Graves Registration Division between October 1947 and January 1949.

Mecklenburg County WWII Memorial

The 20-foot-tall granite WWII monument was sponsored by the Mecklenburg County Gold Star Mother's Club, Inc., and was completed in 1949. Wing-like panels stretching out from both sides of the tower list the names of the soldiers from Mecklenburg County who died during the war.

Captain Jack

The Spirit of Mecklenburg honors young tavern owner Captain James Jack, who in May 1775 volunteered to take the Mecklenburg Declaration of Independence to the Continental Congress in Philadelphia. The treasonous documents declared that Charlotte-towne and Mecklenburg County were no longer under British rule.

Martin Luther King, Jr. Memorial

Located in Uptown's Marshall Park, the 8-foot-tall, bronze statue pays homage to one of America's most-influential Civil Rights activists. The monument was unveiled during a ceremony on April 5, 1980, at which Reverend Martin Luther King Sr., Governor Jim Hunt, and statue creator Selma Burke addressed attendees.

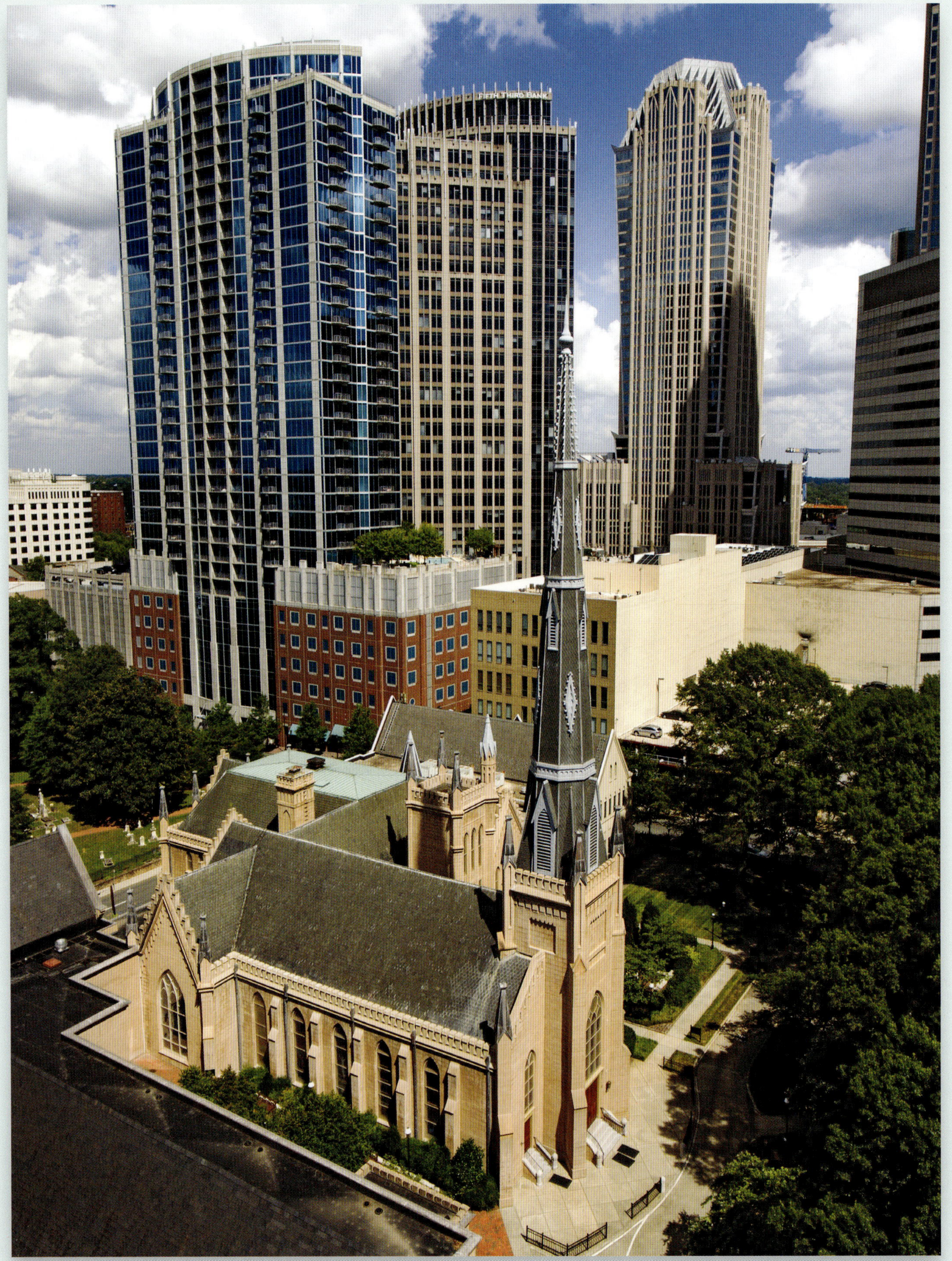
FIFTH THIRD BANK

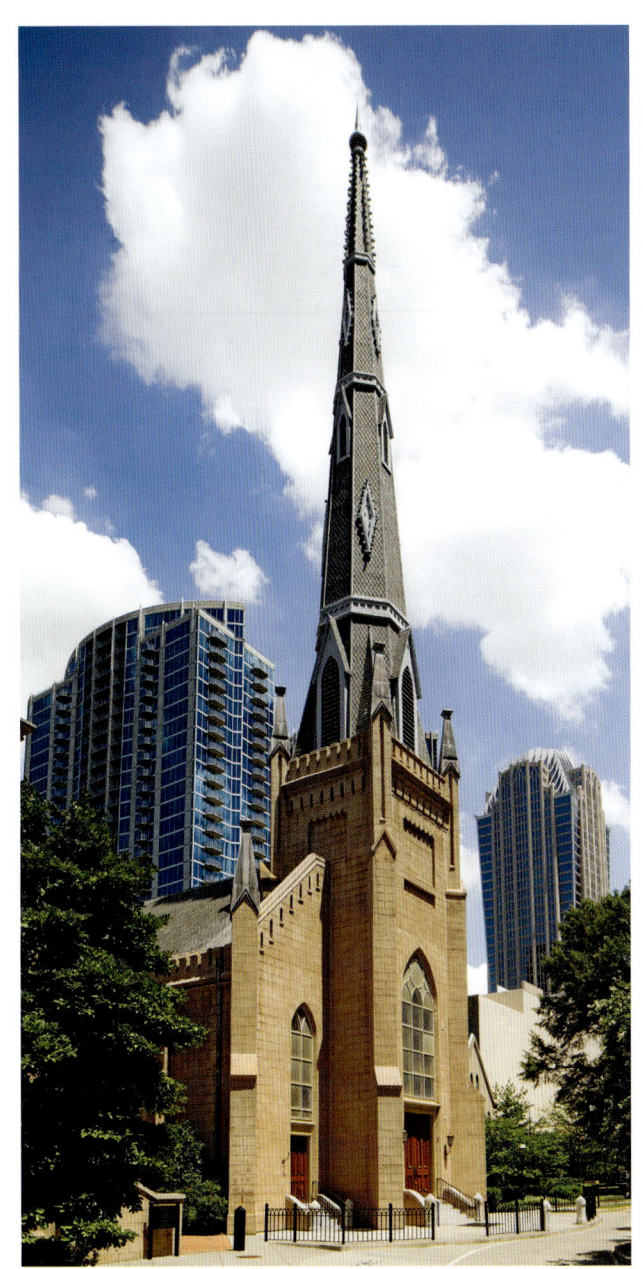

First Presbyterian Church
(left and opposite)

The height of Charlotte's Uptown buildings has grown dramatically since the First Presbyterian Church was completed in 1857 along W. Trade Street. The one-story, Gothic Revival-style stuccoed brick building was added to the National Register of Historic Places in 1982.

First United Methodist Church *(right)*

Also located in Uptown Charlotte stands the First United Methodist Church, which was completed in 1928. This architecturally stunning structure made history in April 2016 when two Charlotte men became the first same-sex couple to publicly marry in a United Methodist Church.

St. Mary's Chapel

A congregation of 100 people can barely squeeze into the tiny, but well known, St. Mary's Chapel on E. Third Street, located just outside of the I-277 beltway that defines Uptown. Operated by Mecklenburg County Park and Recreation department, the quaint chapel, with its appealing charm, is a popular venue for weddings.

St. Peter's Episcopal Church

Organized in 1834, St. Peter's Episcopal Church was the first Episcopal Church in Charlotte. The current structure, at West Seventh and North Tryon streets, was completed in 1895. St. Peter's has impacted the community since the Civil War, when the church raised funds to provide Bibles and prayer books for soldiers.

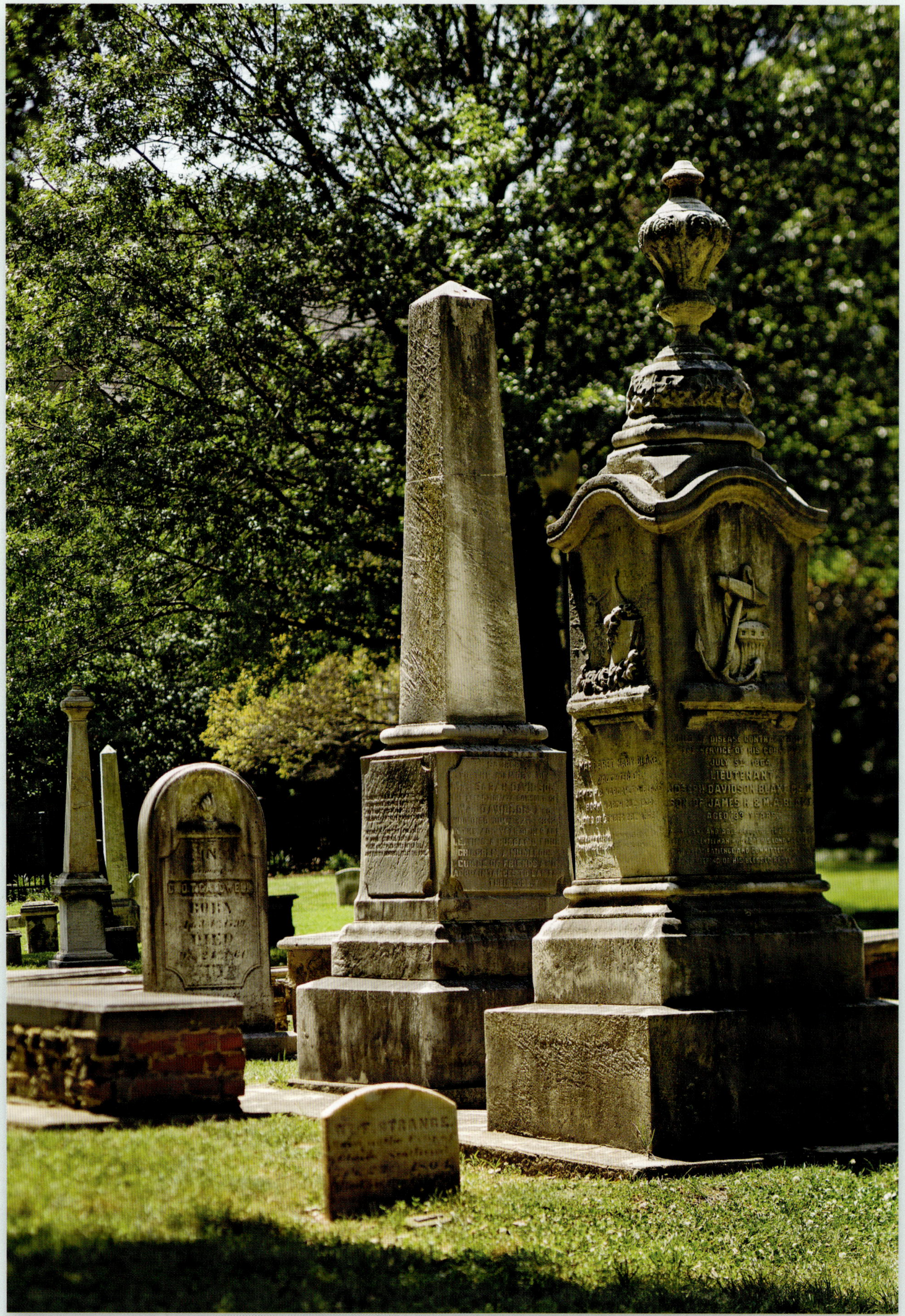

LIEUTENANT
BORN
DIED

Old Settlers' Cemetery

(above, right, and opposite)

This city-owned cemetery, located right in the center of Charlotte, was the city's first municipal burial ground. It contains the graves of many early settlers and has gravesites dating from 1776 to 1884. Today, the cemetery is a centerpiece of the Fourth Ward Historic District.

Billy Graham Library *(top and opposite)*

The 40,000-square-foot structure is a museum and library that documents the life and ministry of evangelist Billy Graham. Located on the grounds of the Billy Graham Evangelistic Association's international headquarters, it also includes multi-media displays and recreations of historic moments in Billy Graham's life and ministry.

Billy Graham Library at Christmas *(bottom)*

The Billy Graham Library attracts thousands of visitors each December for its annual Christmas at the Library event, which includes horse-drawn carriage rides, a live nativity, light displays, Christmas caroling, and more. The library opened in 2007.

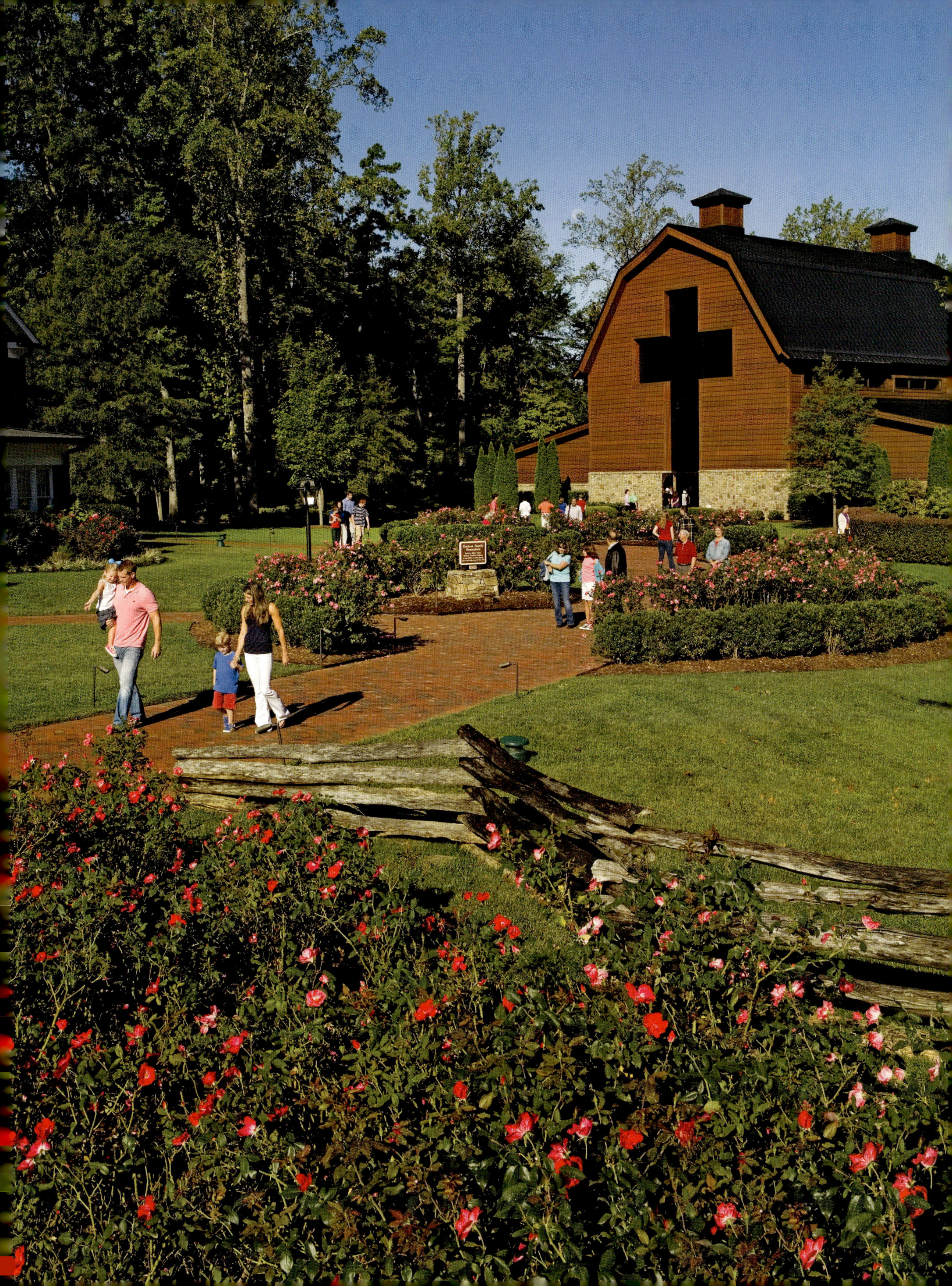

Springtime (above)

Sitting on a covered porch, like the one on Fourth Ward's Eastlake Cottage, is a perfectly relaxing way to enjoy spring in Charlotte. Spring comes early to Mecklenburg County, where the daffodils and tulips frequently bloom before March.

Center of the Known World (opposite)

Within The Green in Uptown, a wooden post features brightly colored arrows that point to 11 other cities also named Charlotte. Contemporary artist Gary Sweeney, based in San Antonio, Texas, created the piece with the approximate direction of the locales identified as well as the distance to each.

CHARLOTTE TENNESSEE 470 MILES
CHARLOTTE MAINE 1164 MILES
CHARLOTTE TEXAS 1275 MILES
CHARLOTTE VERMONT 893 MILES
CHARLOTTE IOWA 940 MILES
CHARLOTTE WATERS, AUSTRALIA 9,975 MILES
CHARLOTTE HALL, MARYLAND 390 MILES
CHARLOTTE NORTH CAROLINA
THE CENTER OF THE KNOWN WORLD!

Fourth Ward Park *(above)*

Lush greens beckon visitors to the Fourth Ward Park, a 3-acre neighborhood expanse that stretches between Sixth and Eighth streets in Uptown. The park features walking trails, a playground, decorative water fountains, and countless plantings.

Ornate Embellishment *(left)*

An artistic figure adorns the exterior of a home in the Fourth Ward. The historic district is located directly north of the intersection of Trade and Tryon streets. Grand Victorian homes, with their distinct architectural details, lush, colorful gardens, and ornate fences, line the quiet streets of this mostly residential area.

Fourth Ward

Standing stately within the confines of its signature, ornate wrought iron fence, the Berryhill House, a Victorian Italianate-style home built in 1884, might be the most-photographed home in the Fourth Ward. The historic house features 8-foot-tall windows, corniced eaves, a square roof turret, and a wrap-around veranda.

76

Duke Mansion *(opposite top and bottom)*

Built in 1915 and tripled in size by James B. Duke, the home's most-famous owner, the Duke Mansion is now operated as a nonprofit whose proceeds are used to preserve and protect the property. The property hosts meetings and weddings and has 20 overnight guest rooms.

Historic Rosedale Plantation *(above)*

Also known as "Frew's Folly," the Historic Rosedale Plantation house is a 2.5-story Federal-style dwelling built in 1807. Today, the plantation is a non-profit dedicated to preserving and promoting the heritage of the Catawba River Valley Region.

VanLandingham Estate

(above, left, and opposite)

Brick pathways and manicured gardens welcome visitors to the VanLandingham Estate, an historic inn/bed and breakfast located in Plaza Midwood. Built in 1913, the estate is listed on the National Register of Historic Places.

VanLandingham Estate *(pages 80-81)*

VanLandingham Estate's four acres of grounds feature the oldest premier gardens in Mecklenburg County as well as a distinctive, two-story bungalow-style home originally built with wood shingles. The home was part of a widespread revolt in the 1900s against the fussiness of Victorian style homes.

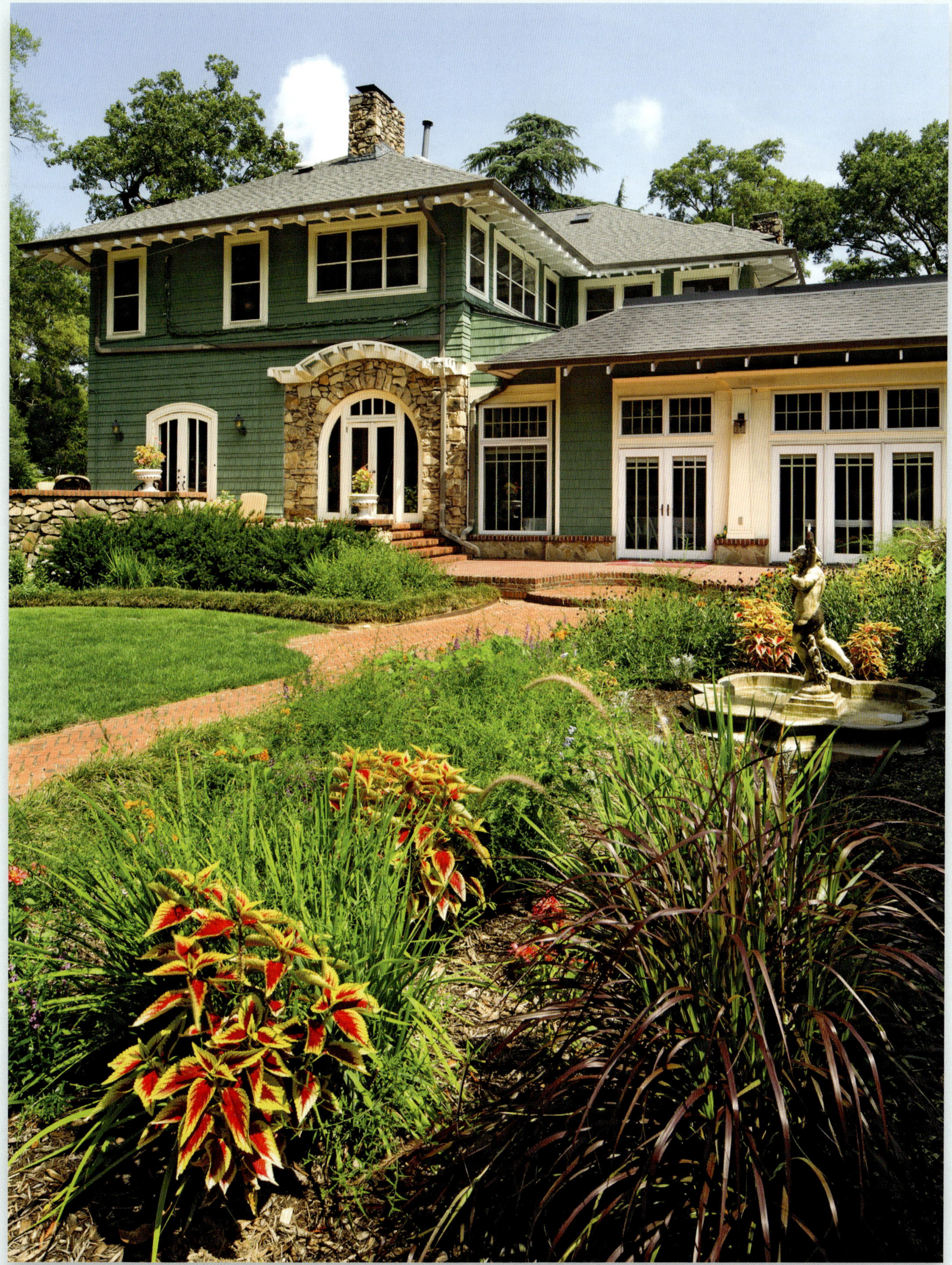

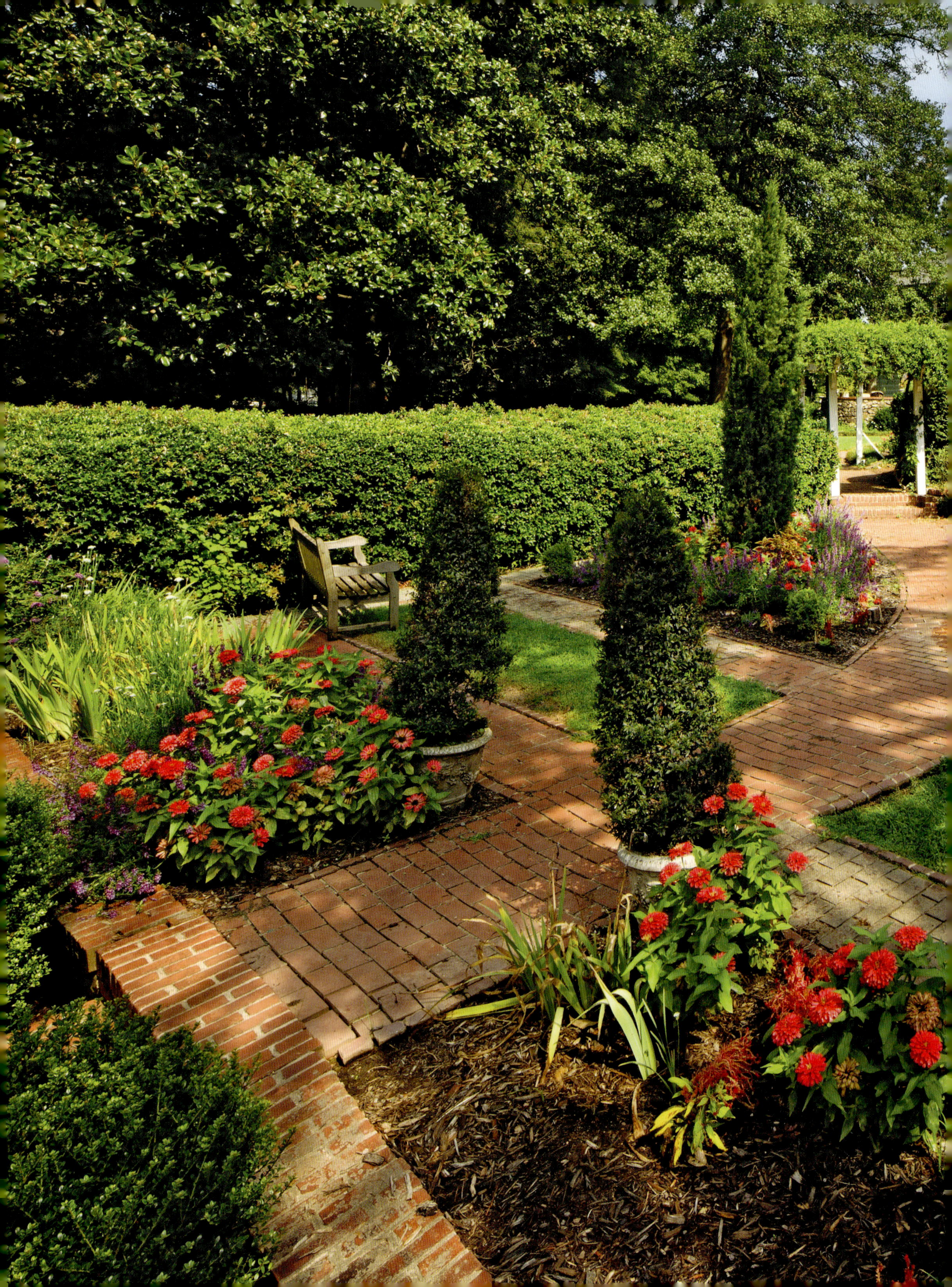

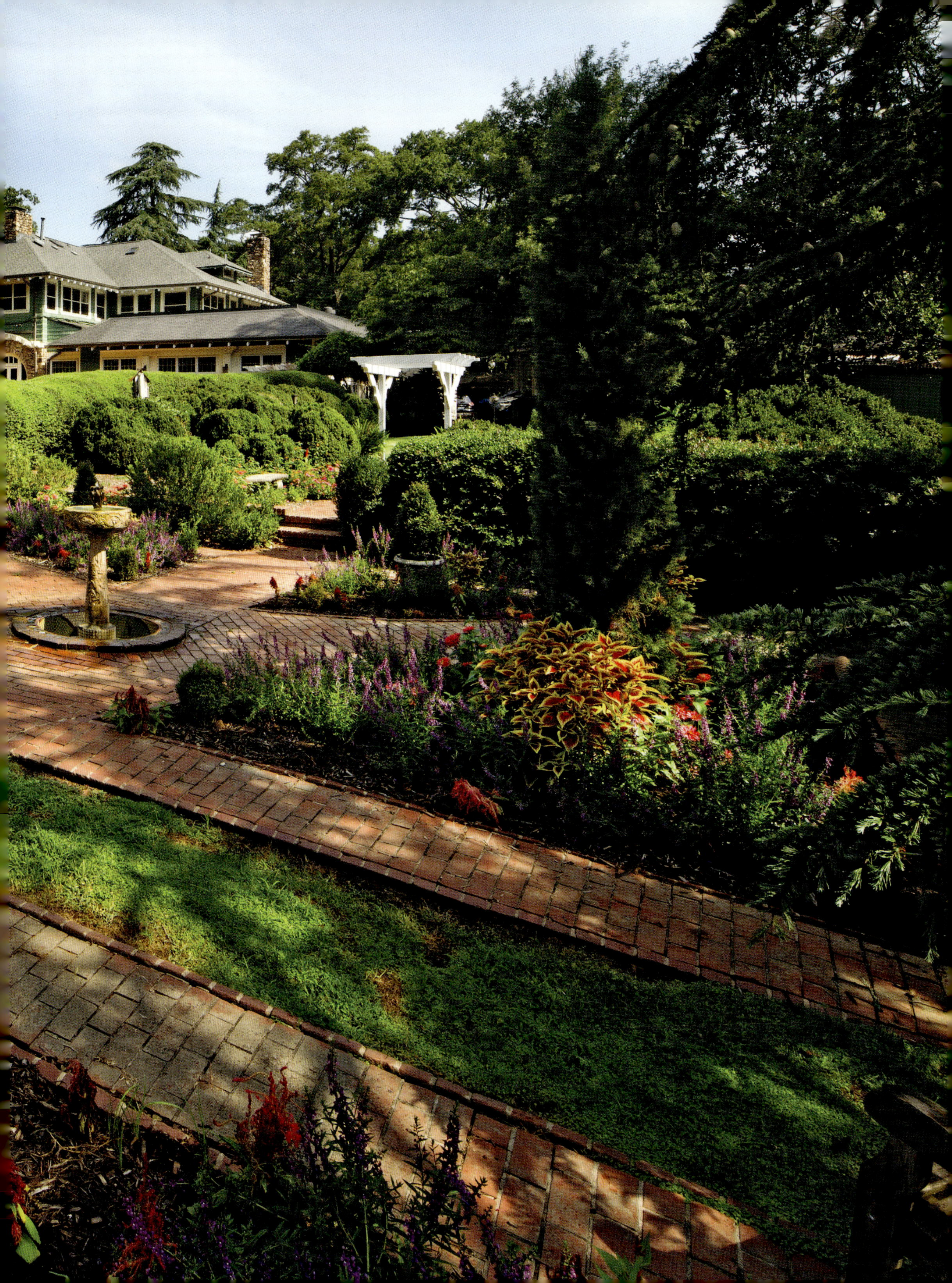

Wing Haven Gardens
(above, left, and opposite)

This three-acre haven includes peaceful pathways, two public gardens, and a special sanctuary for birds and wildlife. In addition to serving its mission of cultivating sanctuary in nature, environmental stewardship and the legacy of Southern horticulture, it is a garden writer's living laboratory.

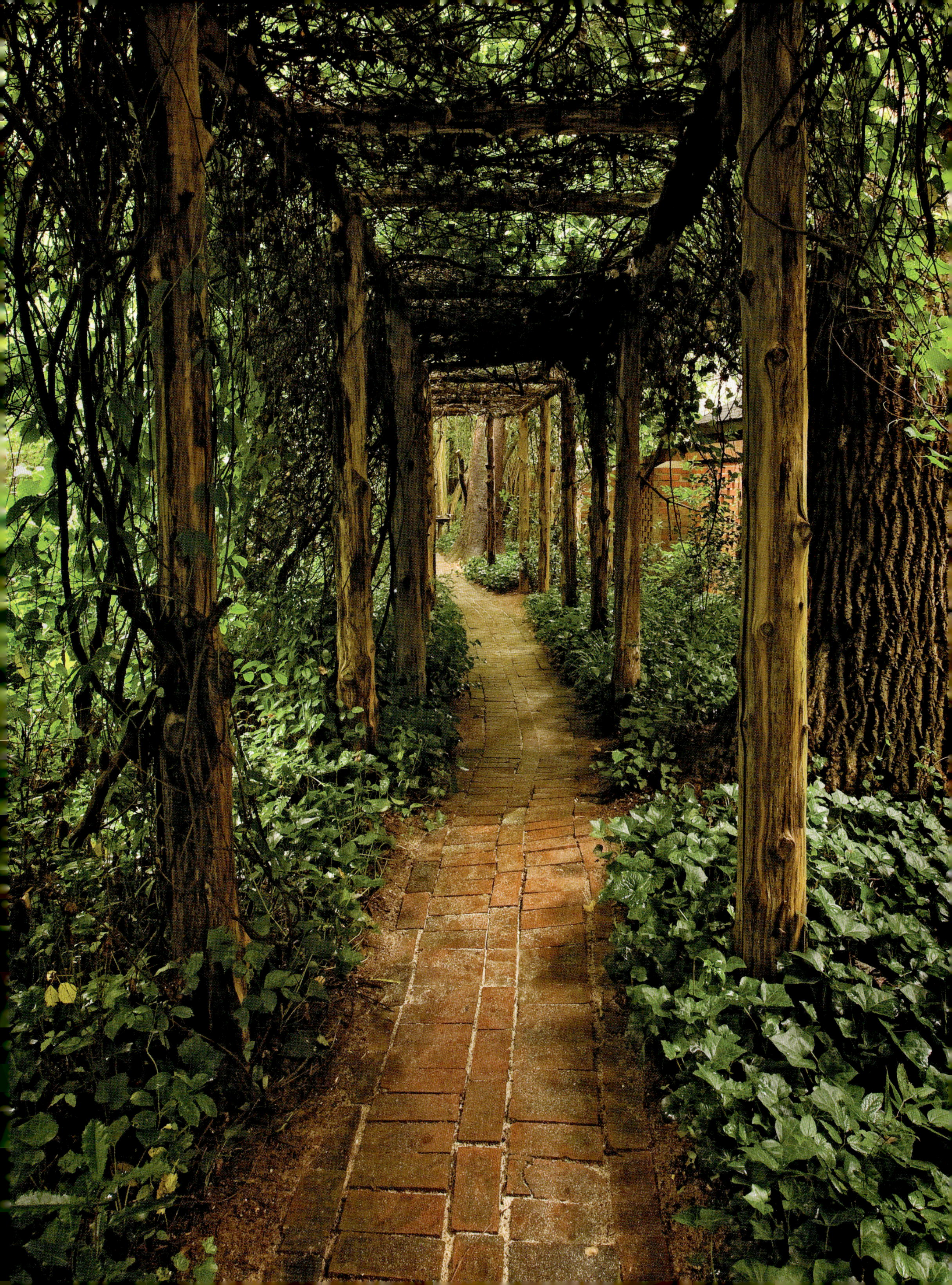

84

Wells Fargo History Museum
(opposite top and bottom)

The Wells Fargo History Museum is located adjacent to the Levine Center for the Arts. The museum highlights the days of gold mining in North Carolina and the beginnings of Charlotte's Wachovia Bank, which merged with Wells Fargo in 2008.

Concord Statecoach *(above)*

A mid-19th-century Concord stagecoach, which visitors are allowed to climb aboard, is a favorite exhibit at the Wells Fargo History Museum. Other exhibits include an interactive telegraph, a recreated underground mine tunnel, gold nuggets, and rare coins. Museum admission is free.

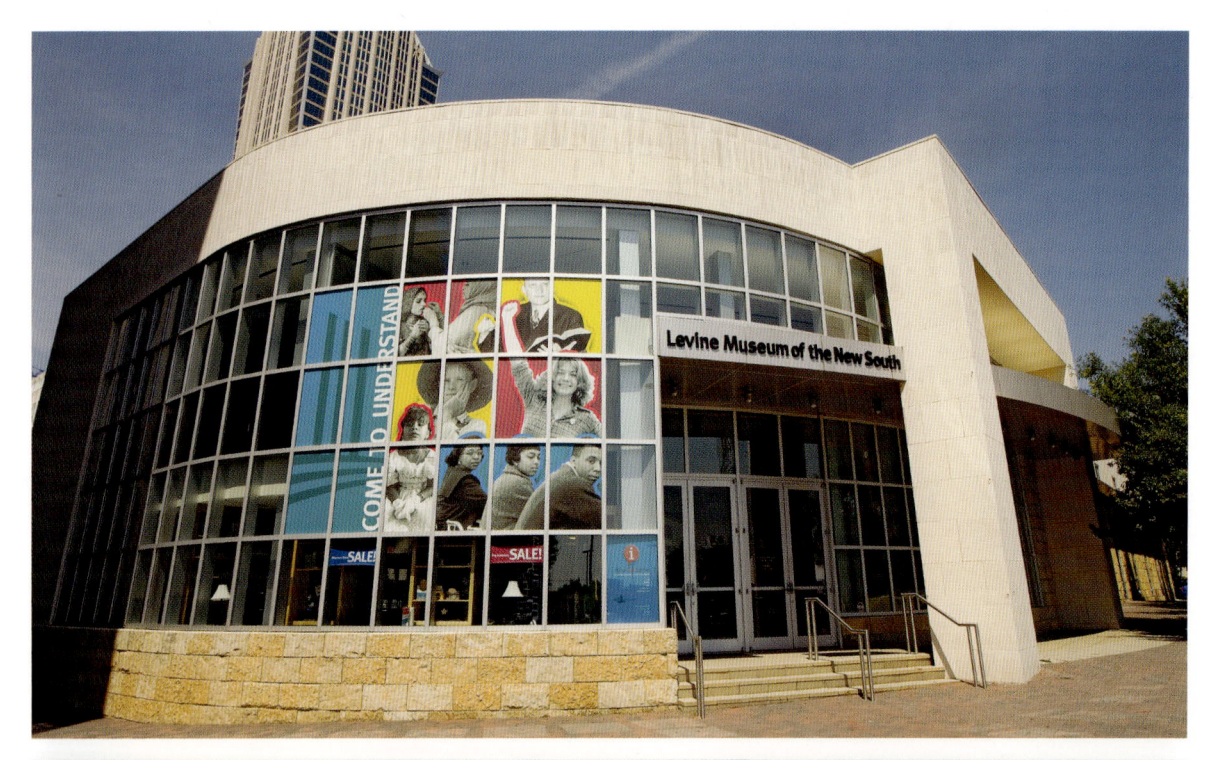

Levine Museum of the New South
(top and bottom)

This interactive museum provides a comprehensive interpretation of post-Civil War southern history from 1865 to today. The museum is best known for its interactive Cotton Fields to Skyscrapers permanent exhibit, in which visitors can watch the process of turning seed cotton into textiles.

ImaginOn *(opposite and pages 88–89)*

Part public library, part theatre and fully a place that encourages learning, ImaginOn: The Joe & Joan Martin Center is a one-of-a-kind youth destination. Located in the heart of Uptown, this is a unique place where "young people learn in many ways, through all five senses and from the page to the stage."

87

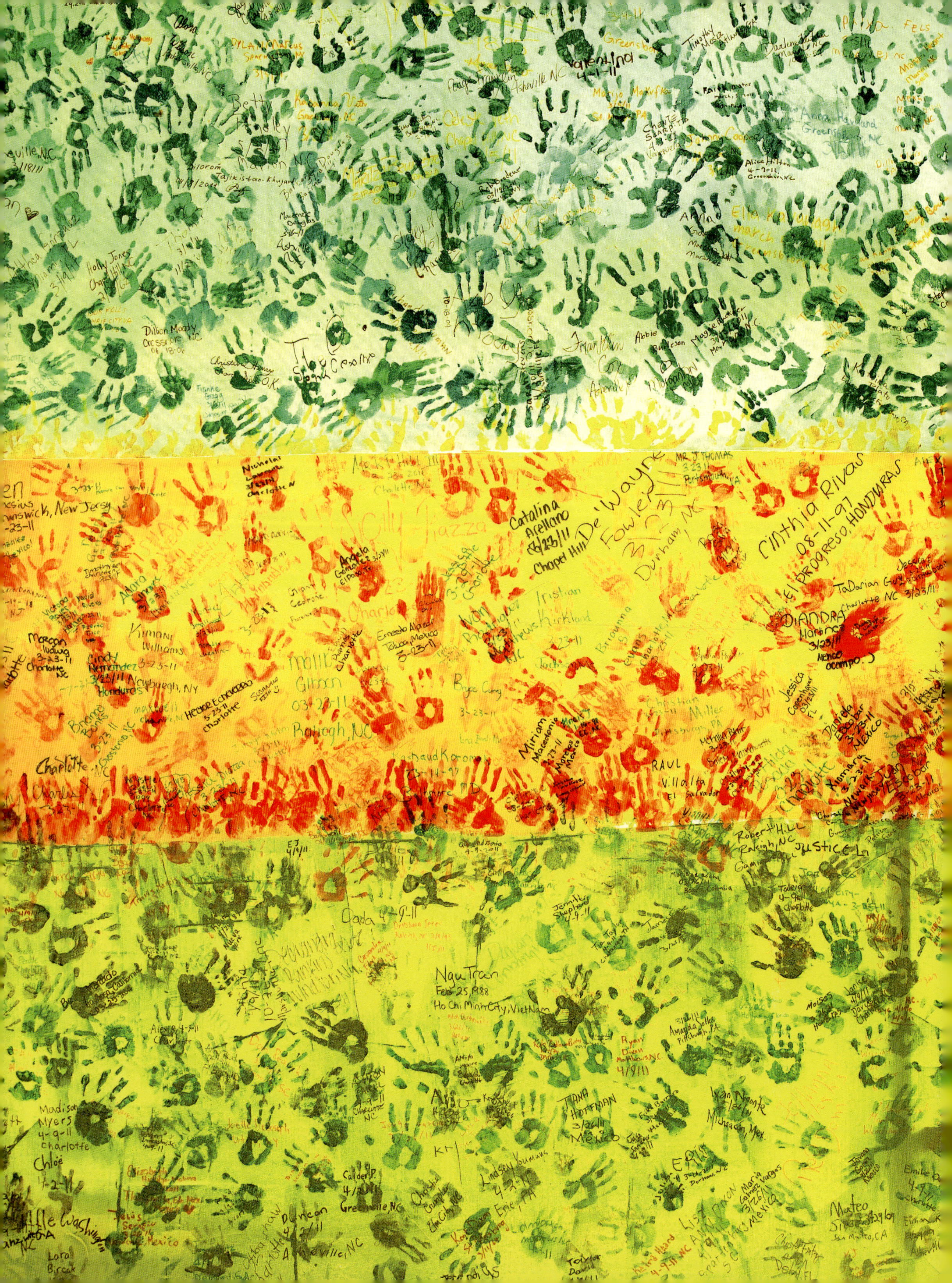

Antonio wilson
03/23/2011
charlotte
Chelsea
Smith
03/23/2011
Charlotte
Juan Peralta
3-23-11
New York
Christopher
Gomez
Honduras Tela
Dominique
LACY
3/23/11
Florence, SC
Steven Delgado
Francisco Oaxaca
Yona
chris

Carolinas Aviation Museum

(top and bottom)

Located on the grounds of the Charlotte Douglas International Airport, the Carolinas Aviation Museum features the history of commercial, civil, military, and helicopter flight. Along with more than 50 planes and helicopters, exhibits include uniforms, signage, manuals, and more.

Miracle on the Hudson

The Carolinas Aviation Museum is home to the Miracle on the Hudson plane, US Airways Flight 1549 that was en route to Charlotte/Douglas International Airport when it successfully landed in New York's Hudson River after striking a flock of Canada geese six minutes after taking off from LaGuardia Airport.

El Dominante *(above)*

El Dominante, meaning the dominant one, was captured during the Spanish-American war and presented to the City of Charlotte in 1900 by President William McKinley. This 250-year-old cannon contributes to the Charlotte Museum of History in protecting the rich heritage of this ever-changing city.

American Freedom Bell *(left)*

Weighing seven tons and spanning seven feet in height and width, the museum's American Freedom Bell symbolizes the patriotic heritage of the people of Charlotte and Mecklenburg County. The bell is located between the Hezekiah Alexander Homesite and the Charlotte Museum of History.

Discovery Place Nature (above)

Small hands take a refreshing retreat from electronic gadgetry at Discovery Place Nature. Part of four hands-on museums networked across the Charlotte metro region, Discovery Place Nature is located on the edge of Freedom Park, between historic Dilworth and the Myers Park community.

Fort Wild (right)

Fort Wild at Discovery Place Nature is a unique experience that encourages unstructured play and exploration of nature. The area was generously funded by the National Wildlife Federation to show families how to create outdoor play spaces from natural elements that can be found in their own backyards.

The Mint Museum

A visitor to The Mint Museum examines *Threshold*, a 26-foot-long stacked and molded glass sculpture by artist Danny Lane. The museum opened in 2010 in a 145,000-square-foot, five-story building in Uptown. A second location, the Mint Museum Randolph, is located in Charlotte's Eastover neighborhood.

Discovery Place Science
(above and right)

Part of a network of four hands-on museums, Discovery Place Science is the museum's crown jewel for fun with science. At World Alive, visitors can touch live animals and explore the wonders of the world.

95

96

Discovery Place Science
(opposite top and bottom)

Whether mesmerized by jellyfish or witnessing chemistry in action, Discovery Place Science wants visitors up close and, when possible, hands on. Each year more than 825,000 visitors come to see interactive activities, thrilling experiments, an IMAX Dome Theatre, and ever-changing exhibits.

Hands-On Learning
(top and bottom)

Visitors make exaggerated movements in the museum's *Think It Up* exhibit *Sound Space* display (top), which translates body movements into sound. In the *Making Shelter* exhibit (bottom) visitors channel their inner survivalist to build forts using PVC pipe, posts, and mesh fabric.

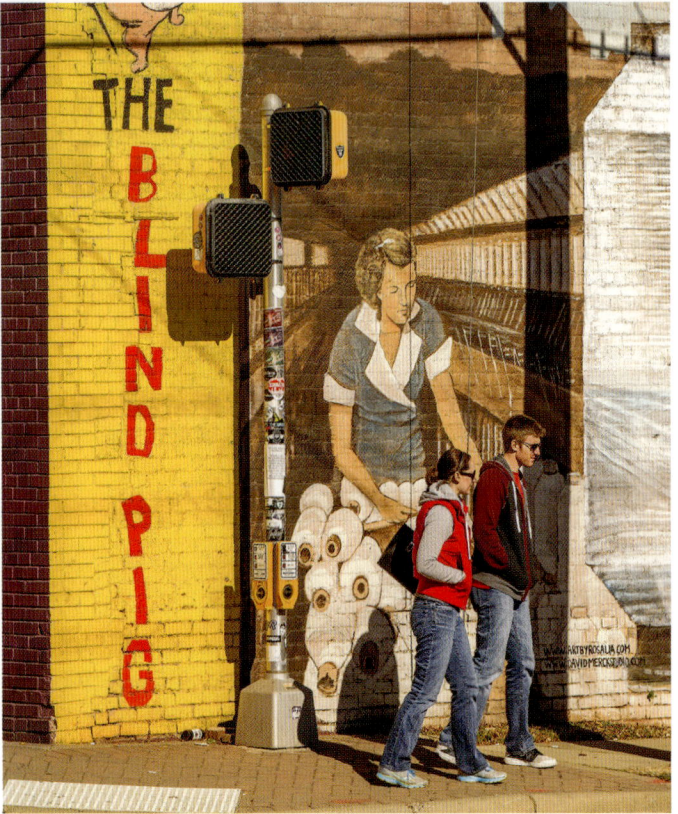

NoDa Charlotte Historic Arts District *(above)*

Artist William Puckett made no commission for NoDa mural *Als Ich Chan: A Tribute to NoDa*. The 1,200-square-foot piece features 270 neighborhood residents in a group portrait. Puckett spent 18 months on the project, located on the wall of local tavern Jack Beagle's, to encourage people to embrace art.

NoDa *(left)*

NoDa, short for "North Davidson," is a popular arts district located about one mile northeast of Uptown. Formerly a neighborhood of residences for local textile manufacturing and mill workers, NoDa evolved into a center for arts and entertainment, including a gallery crawl, music venues, and restaurants.

NoDa *(above and right)*

Roughly two dozen murals now adorn the outside walls of NoDa buildings, helping the NoDa neighborhood emphasize its artsy focus. And, more murals are expected to come. In addition to letting local artists get creative, the murals remind viewers of Charlotte's history and encourage visitors to embrace public art.

99

Charlotte Summer Pops Series

Since 1983, the Charlotte Symphony has brought music to the masses by performing under the stars during its Summer Pops program. The five-concert summer series takes place at Symphony Park at SouthPark Mall. The non-profit symphony was founded in 1932.

Alive After 5 *(above and right)*

Held in multiple locations around Charlotte, the annual Alive After Five celebration kick-starts the weekend in style. The weekly happy hour and free entertainment usually runs spring through fall. Photos show the after-work crowd at Alive After 5 at Piedmont Town Center in SouthPark.

101

Christmas Lights

A white-light-covered Christmas tree surrounded by glistening reindeer herald the winter holiday season to the city. From displays to special events, visitors are enchanted throughout the city with the glow of sparking lights and an assortment of things to do.

First Night

First Night Charlotte, also known as CLT New Year's Eve, is a family-friendly New Year's Eve celebration that often moves to a new Uptown location each year. Here, Charlotteans welcome in the new year with fireworks and celebrations at Romare Bearden Park.

First Night *(left and right)*

Fireworks explode with vibrant bursts of color over the Firebird statue located on the plaza at the Bechtler Museum of Modern Art during First Night Charlotte. Earlier in the day, jugglers, musicians, magicians, and hoop dancers (Vivian "Spiral" Hancock seen here) entertain attendees to this popular event.

First Night *(above and pages 106–107)*

Live music, food, and activities attract more than 75,000 people each year to one of the biggest events in the Southeast. A family-friendly, alcohol-free event, the count down to the new year culminates at midnight with the raising of the Queen City Crown and an amazing fireworks display.

NEW YEAR'S EVE
WBTV
FIRST
NIGHT
CHARLOTTE
WBTV
FIRST
NIGHT
CHARLOTTE
Duke Energy
ENTERTAINMENT STAGE
ally

Novant Health Thanksgiving Day Parade *(above and right)*

More than 100,000 people gather along Tryon Street each November for the annual Novant Health Thanksgiving Day Parade, a tradition that kicks off the official start of the Christmas season for many Charlotteans. Multiple marching bands from across the region participate.

Dragon Boat Festival *(above and left)*

The head of a colorful beast adorns the bow of a dragon boat and leads racers during the annual Charlotte Dragon Boat Festival Races on Lake Norman. The race and Charlotte Asian Festival are held each spring at Ramsey Creek Park in Cornelius, North Carolina, just 20 miles north of Charlotte.

Carowinds *(above and right)*

Carolina Cobra and Fury 325 roller coasters twist and zoom riders at Carowinds, a 112-acre combination amusement park and water park. The park is home to 13 world-famous roller coasters and two of the tallest coasters in North America.

US National Whitewater Center
(above, left, and opposite)

The 1100-acre USNWC offers outdoor activities for all ages. The center's signature feature is the recirculating artificial whitewater river, which can be adjusted for rafting and kayaking by people of all skill levels. The center's land activities include climbing, rope courses, ziplines, and trails.

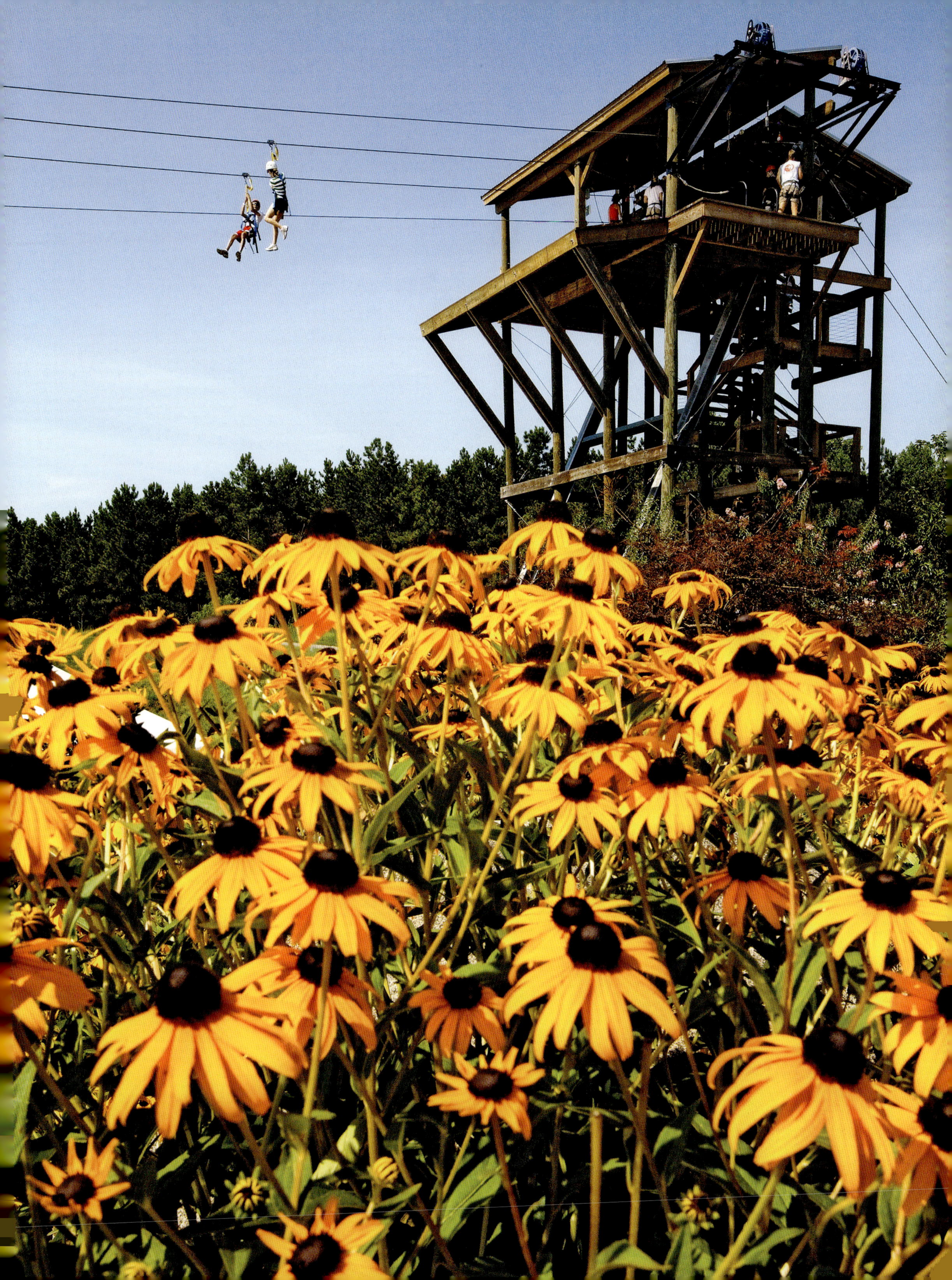

116

Queen's Cup (opposite top and bottom)

Each April, riders and spectators head to the Piedmont countryside to watch athletic thoroughbred horses clear obstacles as jockeys show off their skills in brightly colored silks. Participants turn heads with creative, eye-catching hats made or purchased specifically for the Queen's Cup Steeplechase.

Queen's Cup (top and bottom)

Numerous non-racing activities are part of the Queen's Cup celebration, including opening ceremonies with a Walking of the Hounds demonstration by Mecklenburg Hounds. However, the most-anticipated events are the four steeplechase races, during which horses and riders strive to safely clear fences and water features.

12
48
OFFICIAL
LOWES
KOBALT TOOLS
EAGLE
GOODYEAR

Coca-Cola 600
CHARLOTTE
MOTOR SPEEDWAY

Coca Cola 600 *(opposite top and bottom)*

The Charlotte Motor Speedway is home to the Coca-Cola 600, the 600-mile NASCAR Sprint Cup Series race held Memorial Day weekend. This race is the longest race on the NASCAR circuit. Drivers begin racing in sunlight and finish under dark skies and speedway lights.

NASCAR Hall of Fame *(above)*

Many NASCAR-loving Carolinians celebrated when Charlotte was selected to be the home of the NASCAR Hall of Fame. The 150,000-square-foot hall opened in 2010 as an interactive entertainment attraction honoring the history and heritage of NASCAR. The hall includes artifacts, exhibits, and a 278-person theater.

BB&T BallPark *(top and bottom)*

In 2014, Charlotte brought the sport of baseball Uptown when it opened the BB&T Ballpark as the new home of the Charlotte Knights, a Triple-A minor league team in the International League. The Knights had been based in Fort Mill, South Carolina, about 30 miles south of Uptown.

BB&T BallPark

Surrounded by skyscrapers, BB&T Ballpark sports a big league backdrop. Ballparks don't get much more urban than that. The stadium holds up to 10,200 spectators and hosts public and private events in addition to the national pastime.

Carolina Panthers (above and left)

The Carolina Panthers became the National Football League's 29th franchise team in 1993. The team was established by Jerry Richardson, only the second former professional football player to own an NFL franchise team. Now a formidable NFL opponent, the Panthers played their first game in 1995.

Bank of America Stadium *(above)*

Bank of America Stadium is one of the few stadiums owned by the team that plays in it. Completed in 1996, the nearly 75,500-seat stadium was renovated in the 2014, 2015 and 2016 off seasons to improve the fan experience through state-of-the-art technology and enhanced design.

Skyline with Stadium *(pages 124-125)*

Bank of America stadium and adjacent practice fields sit on 33 acres on the southwest edge of Uptown. In addition to being home to the Carolina Panthers, Bank of America Stadium has hosted several college championship football games, multiple international soccer matches, and a four-day Billy Graham crusade.

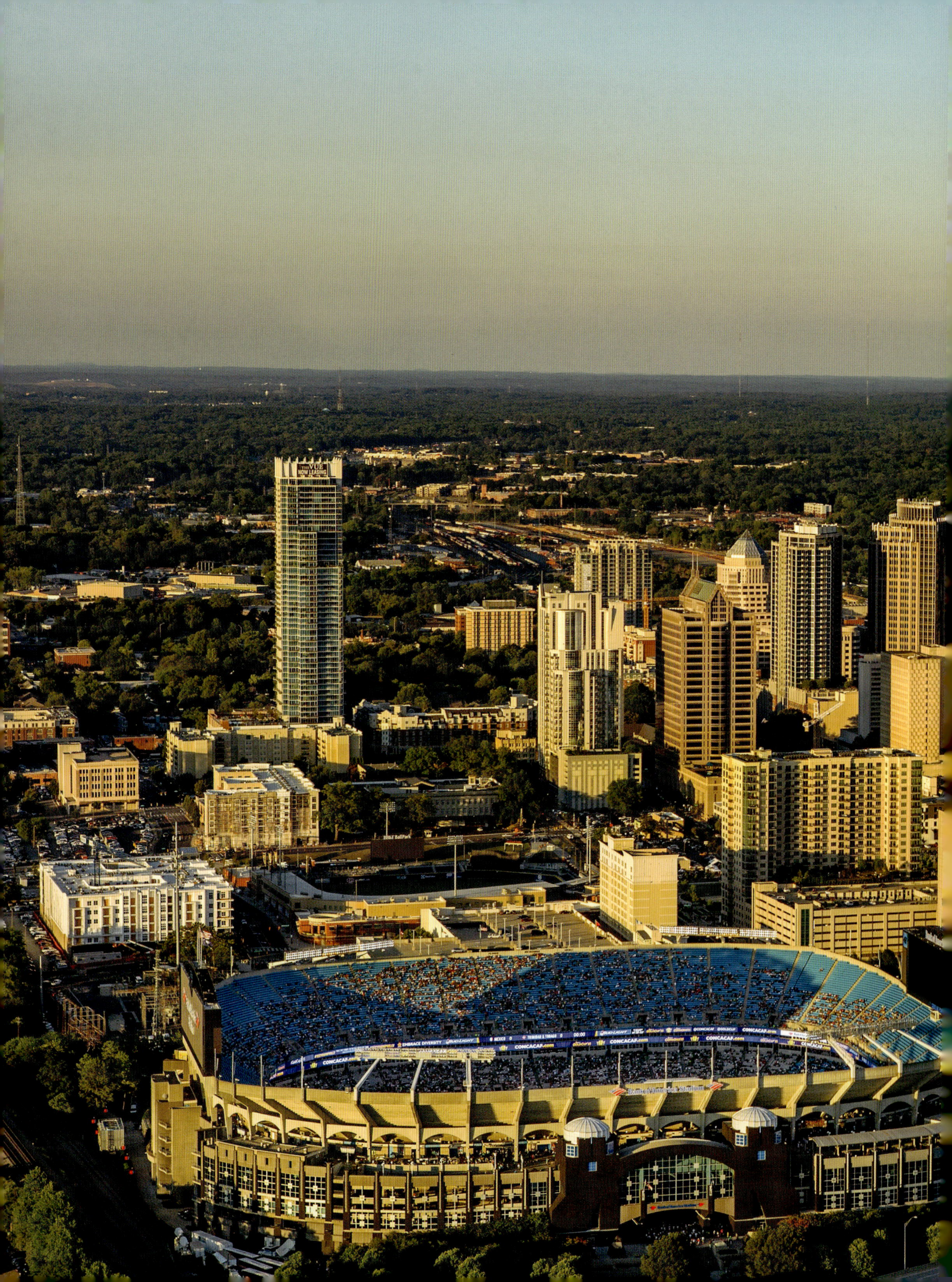
THE VUE
NOW LEASING

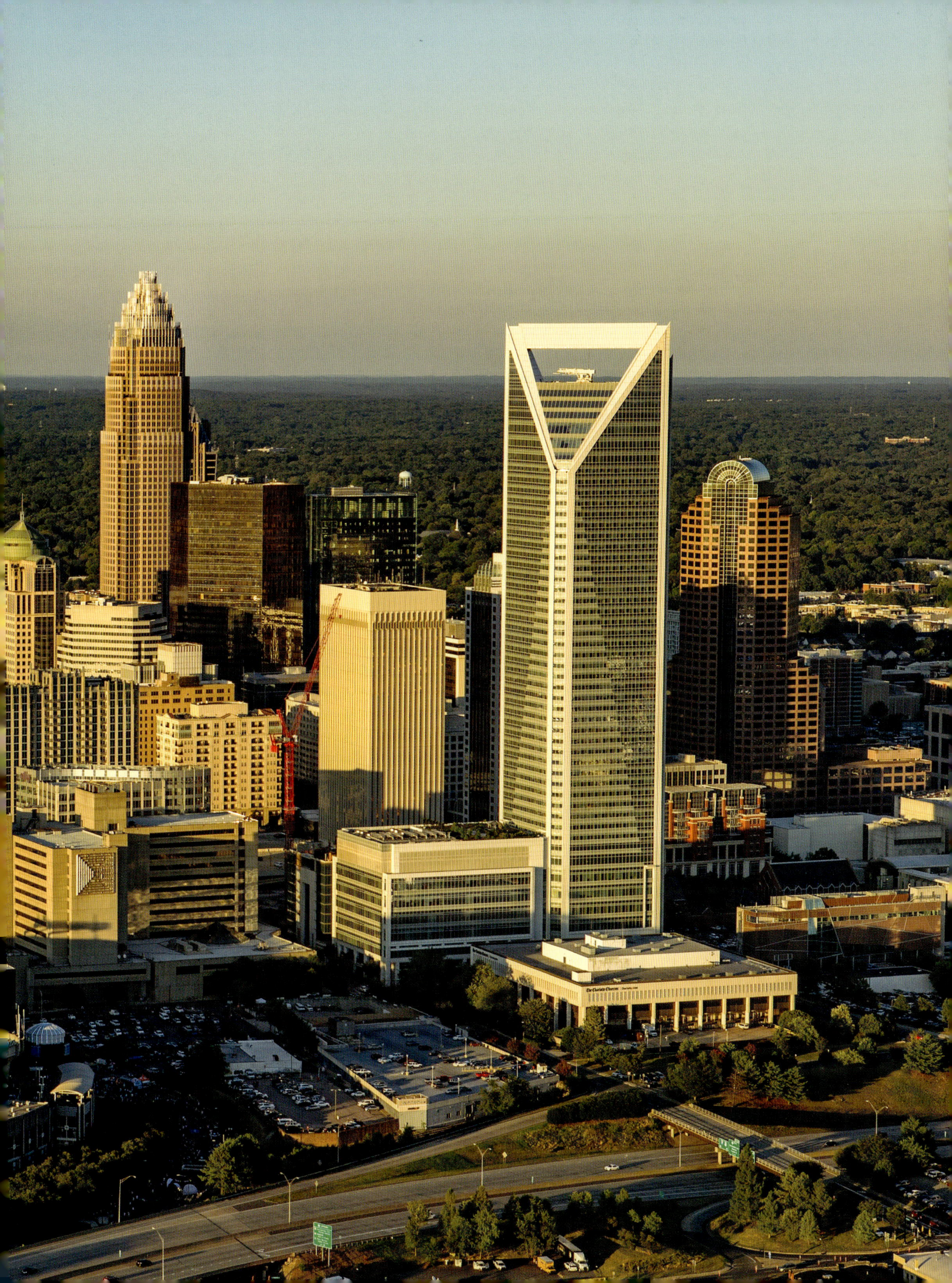

Fourth of July Spectacular
(top and bottom)

Each Independence Day, Charlotte hosts one of the largest fireworks displays in the Southeast. For many years, Memorial Stadium was the center of the July 4th activities, and fireworks were shot off the tops of nearby buildings.

Baseball, Fireworks, and Fun

Baseball, fireworks, and fun came together at the BB&T Ballpark, the city's annual Fourth of July fireworks celebration. The ballpark is home base for other fireworks celebrations, including when Charlotte rings in the New Year.

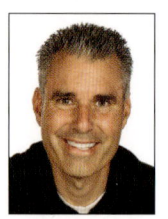

For more than 25 years, award-winning photojournalist **Patrick Schneider** has captivated audiences with his distinctive shooting style. Now, as increasingly more Fortune 500 companies hire trained photojournalists to help them tell their stories, Schneider's talent is keeping him in the demand of marketing teams, creative directors, and corporate communications staffs in Charlotte and around the world. Visit PatrickSchneiderPhoto.com to see more of Patrick's work.

Lore Postman Schneider is a former newspaper business reporter who now uses her talents to help businesses and individuals tell their stories in ways that drive sales, spark engagement, create ambassadors, and cultivate connections. As partners at home and with work, Lore and Patrick are full-service storytellers who engage audiences through words, photos, podcasts, videos, animation, multimedia, and more.